Imran
About Allah

Sajda Nazlee

Ta-Ha Publishers Ltd.
1 Wynne Road,
London, SW9 0BB

Copyright © 1414/1994 Taha Publishers Ltd.
First Published January 1994
Reprinted 9 times 1995-2003

Second Rrevised edition 1425AH / August 2004 CE

Published by:
Ta-Ha Publishers Ltd.
1 Wynne Road
London SW9 0BB

Website: http://www.taha.co.uk
Email: sales@taha.co.uk

Written by: Sajda Nazlee
Edited by: Abdassamad Clarke
General Editor: Dr Abia Afsar-Siddiqui
Design and typesetting by: M. S. Suffee
Illustrated by: M. Ishaq

A catalogue record of this book is available from the British Library.

ISBN 1 842000 63 2

Printed and bound by: De-Luxe Printers, London Ltd.
245a, Acton Lane, London NW10 7NR

Imran Learns About ALLAH

Imran was walking home from school on a summer afternoon with his cousin and best friend, Uthman. It was a wonderful baking hot day. Both boys decided to take the long route home through the outskirts of the town. As they walked, they came across an enormous house with a magnificent, great big garden.

In the garden there were six apple trees loaded with beautiful rosy red apples.

"What an amazing garden! What delicious looking apples!" exclaimed Imran. He stared at the apples. Both boys pressed their faces against the gates of the garden. They peered through at those tempting apples.

"I'm sure they're really juicy," said Uthman. He turned his big green eyes towards his friend and rubbed his tummy. Imran was looking far ahead into the garden to see what else he could spot.

"I think this is a really interesting garden," mused Imran. He almost pushed his friend out of the way.

He was trying to get a better view from where he was standing.

Both boys agreed that if nobody seemed to be watching, they would have a little tour around the garden. They wanted to find out what more they could discover.

"This must belong to a really rich person," said Imran as he ambled in. Uthman followed him, secretly convinced that the garden belonged to a king.

As they walked further into the garden, to their huge surprise, they came across a swimming pool.

"A swimming pool!" cried Uthman, thrilled to bits. The water looked so cool and refreshing. The pool had a deep end and a shallow end.

Imran and Uthman both loved swimming and were like two fishes in the water.

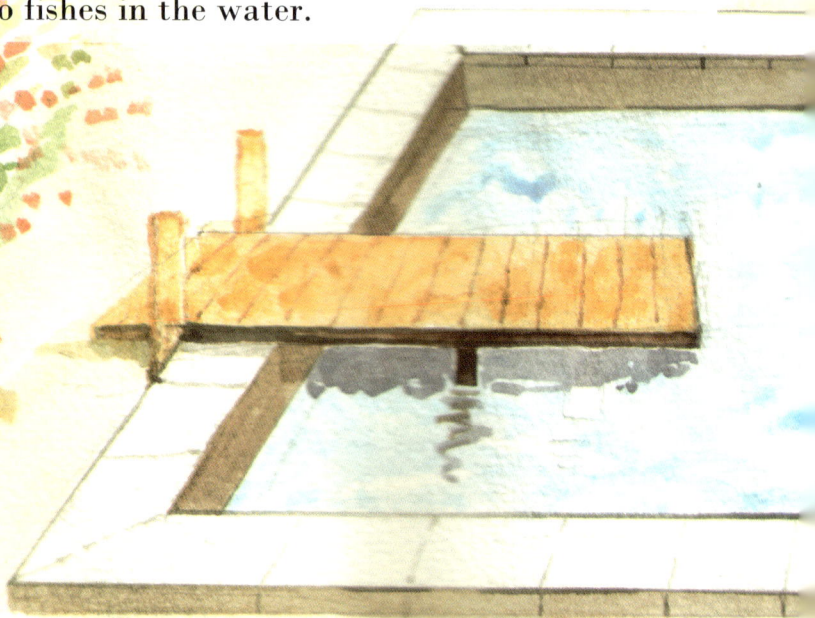

"Come on, Imran! Let's swim in the shallow end," said Uthman, gazing on the water in excitement.

"OK. Nobody is watching us. Let's enjoy ourselves," said Imran, throwing his shirt in the air.

Both boys jumped into the water with a great splash. They found that it was wonderfully cool. First they swam a little and then they played at splashing each other. After they had had enough of swimming, they climbed out of the pool and got dressed without drying themselves.

"I have an idea," said Imran, his eyes wide with excitement, "Let's pluck some apples from one of the trees and eat them them as we play on the see-saw. Then we can dry out at the same time."

So they hurried over to the apple trees. Imran was a little taller than Uthman, and so Uthman used his friend's shoulders to climb on the tree and reach the apples.

Meanwhile, Mr. Ali arrived. He owned the magnificent house and splendid garden. He had been watering some of the flower-beds further down in the garden. He was alarmed to see two boys at his tree. "I wonder what's going on?" he asked himself anxiously.

Imran and Uthman had absolutely no idea at all that Mr. Ali was standing right behind them, watching. They had their back turned to him. The two boys were totally engrossed in carrying out the plan they had hatched. Mr. Ali went on watching the two boys completely silently.

Uthman had learnt the great secret of plucking all fruits, but especially apples. It is important to pluck only the apples which come easily away in your hand and not to pull hard on them. The apples which come away from the tree softly and easily are the ripest and the sweetest of them all.

When he had plucked them, Uthman did something very silly. He dropped the apples behind him forgetting that they would bruise when they fell on the hard ground.

"Uthman, please don't throw the apples too far. They might end up in the swimming pool. I'm nearly dry now. I don't want to go for another dip," said Imran.

"Don't worry, they won't be far behind us," replied Uthman, whose arms were becoming tired also from stretching to reach the best apples. They seemed to be just beyond his reach.

After Uthman had plucked a few apples, he asked Imran, "Are these apples enough?"
"Yes, Yes," said Imran, "Don't pluck any more. We must hurry now before someone sees us." Uthman climbed clumsily down from Imran's shoulders.

Both of them turned around to look for the apples. Imagine their shock to see Mr. Ali standing right there with some apples in his hands! They were lost for words - Mr. Ali was their HEADMASTER! Neither of them could say a word. Their throats were dry. They had swum like fish. Now they stood there with their mouths open like fish.

"Well," said Mr. Ali, breaking the silence, "I think you'd both better come over and talk with me."

Mr. Ali sat himself down on the bench which was beside the swimming pool. Both boys rushed over feeling terrified and dared not look at each other nor Mr. Ali. They had been terribly worried that someone might see them and it had turned out much worse than they had imagined.

"So," began Mr. Ali, looking at both boys from above his glasses, "Did you have a good swim then?"

"Yes-s, w-we..." stuttered Imran, opening and closing his mouth more and more like a fish. "We were really hot so we thought that we should cool ourselves down a bit. We didn't know it was your house, did we Uthman?" Imran looked to Uthman for support, hoping he might say something too but Uthman only looked silently from Imran to Mr. Ali and said nothing.

"I see," said Mr. Ali, looking a little stern, "You thought that nobody was watching you so why not have a good time?"

"Do you not know that you are always being watched by Allah?" said Mr. Ali, sitting both boys down, one on either side of him, "Allah sees you all the time. Whatever you are doing, whenever or wherever, Allah sees everything."

The boys had worried about an adult seeing them but they had never thought at all about Allah seeing them and seeing them all the time and everywhere! Here was something which needed thinking about.

"Sometimes," began Imran, "I hide my brother Faisal's colouring pens under my bed so that I can use them when he falls asleep. Does Allah know where I've hidden the pens and why I've hidden them?"

"Allah knows what we think. He knows all about us no matter where we are. Allah knows where everything is no matter where we hide it," replied Mr. Ali.

"Sometimes I hide my crisps from, Salwa, my sister and eat them under the bedclothes. Does Allah see me eat my crisps?" asked Uthman. Really he was being a little cheeky with his question but Mr. Ali pretended not to notice.

"Of course! You must never think that you are alone. Even though Salwa cannot see you eat your crisps, Allah sees you," said Mr. Ali.

"So that means that when I play hide and seek with Salwa, Allah knows where we are hiding," said Uthman looking up at Mr. Ali. The boys were awash with questions now.

"Can Allah see me even if I hide in my wardrobe where it's really dark or when I turn off the bedroom light with the curtains closed?" asked Imran.

"Allah can see a black ant on a black rock on a pitch black night with no moonlight and plenty of clouds. Allah can see everything everywhere no matter how dark it is. He sees everything all the time at the same time. When you, Uthman, hide your crisps from your sister and you, Imran, hide your pencils from your brother, Allah sees all of you at the same time and the ant on the black rock and everything that is everywhere," explained Mr. Ali seriously.

They couldn't imagine it and so they were really amazed. They were really interested now in what Mr. Ali was telling them. They wanted him to tell them more about Allah. So, Mr. Ali gave Imran and Uthman an apple each, the same apples they had worked so hard to pluck from the tree. Then he began to tell them more about Allah, as they listened intently.

"Allah tells us in the Qur'an that He is able to do all things. He can do anything and everything. All He has to say is 'Be' and it happens. Allah is the Most Powerful and the Most Wise. "

"Allah is the Creator of the heavens and the earth. He made the moon, the sun, the sky and the stars. They all belong to Him. They all obey His laws. The sun comes out and then it is daylight. The sun sets and then it becomes dark and the moon and the stars appear. This is all Allah's doing."

"He made this world and the things in it like the flowers, the trees, the mountains, the birds, the animals and us. He creates them all the time because you can see that there are baby creatures being born all the time."

The boys tried really hard to imagine doing something so huge as changing the night and the day, and creating all the millions of stars so far away, and everything in the world. They could not imagine it at all. It was too big.

"Does anyone help Allah to do all of this hard work?" asked Imran.

"No," said Mr. Ali, "Allah has the power to do anything He wants, exactly whenever He wants."

"Wow! Allah is really great! Really marvellous! He does not need any help in all of this!" said Uthman. He gazed in wonder first at Mr. Ali then at Imran.

"Yes," said Mr. Ali, "Allah has no partners in all of this, no helpers. He does not need to sleep, eat or drink. So you can see that you should really be thankful to Him and worship the One who does all this. You can see how silly it would be to worship anyone else or anything else."

"Does Allah have a mother or a father?" Uthman puzzled aloud. He felt silly for asking the question almost as soon as it came out of his mouth. But he need not have worried because Mr. Ali treated his question seriously and was not a bit angry with him.

"No," said Mr. Ali, shaking his head, "Allah has no mother or father, no brothers or sisters. If you think about it, you will see why that is impossible."

"Allah is the One who has complete and total power over everything," Mr. Ali began, "If there were a brother, sister, mother, father, son or daughter of God then they must also be gods."

"So," Mr. Ali continued, "If there were all these different gods with control over everything, they would have to fight over who had total control over everything."

"So, of course there can only be One God who has control over everything," Uthman realised aloud.

"Allah is alone, He is the only God. A Muslim doesn't believe in any other god with Him," Mr. Ali continued. "A Muslim doesn't worship anything other than Allah because nothing is as marvellous as Him. Allah is Everlasting. He has always existed and always will."

Imran could almost not imagine that Allah could be everlasting. He declared, "Allah has a lot of qualities."

"You're absolutely right, Imran" said Mr. Ali. "In fact, Allah has 99 names or qualities that describe Him. They are called Asma al-Husna which means 'most excellent names'. For example, *Al-Rahman* means 'The Most Merciful' and *Al-Wadud* means 'All-Loving.' These qualities help us to know more about Allah."

After thinking for a minute, Imran asked another question altogether, "Why did Allah make us? Why did He make the world?"

"Allah made the world for us," said Mr. Ali, "Allah wants us to live a happy and peaceful life. He wants us to live as Muslims and He has told us how to do this in his book, the Qur'an. If we live as Muslims, Allah is pleased with us and promises us Heaven where He will reward us for our good actions."

"What do we need to do to be Muslims?" asked Imran.

"There are 5 pillars of Islam which are the main things that make people Muslims. These are saying that there is only One Allah and Muhammad ﷺ is His Messenger, performing regular prayer or Salah, fasting in the month of Ramadan, giving Zakah to those less fortunate than us and the Hajj, or pilgrimage, to Saudi Arabia at least once in our lives."

"To be a good Muslim we must also always listen to our parents and treat them kindly. We must be helpful to everybody, treat our elders and teachers and neighbours well and look after the poor, the orphans and the homeless. We must never hurt anyone's feelings nor be nasty to anyone. Allah doesn't like people who make fun of others and tell lies."

"Does Allah get angry with people who do these bad things?" asked Uthman. He tried to imagine what the anger of the One who made the sun, the moon and the infinite stars could be like. He was rather frightened at the thought.

"Oh yes," answered Mr. Ali, "People who do these naughty things make Allah angry. Allah tells us in the Qur'an that He loves the people who do things which He would like them to do."

Now Imran tried to imagine what the love must be like, of the One who created every living thing on the land, in the oceans and in the air. He just could not imagine how great it would be. But he knew that Allah's love and Allah's anger must be very great indeed.

"Please tell us more about what Allah likes and doesn't like, Mr. Ali," said Imran, looking at his headmaster in excitement.

"Allah wants us to look after old people and help them, like our parents when they become old. He doesn't like us to take things which do not belong to us without asking. He hates us to use bad language," he said.

"Uthman and I never use bad language, do we Uthman?" interrupted Imran.

"I'm pleased to hear it, Imran," said Mr. Ali.

"Is Allah angry with people who do bad things, thinking that Allah doesn't see them?" asked Imran who suddenly remembered just why he and Uthman were sitting with Mr. Ali. He had become really worried because of what he and Uthman had done in Mr. Ali's garden.

"Well yes," replied Mr. Ali, "But the two of you didn't really know that you were doing something which Allah dislikes. I think Allah will forgive you, because I have forgiven you and Allah is more forgiving than me, Allah is the Most Forgiving of all." He added, "Allah is the friend of the believers."Mr. Ali smiled at the two.

"Is Allah really the friend of the believers?" cried Imran in excitement, nearly knocking Mr. Ali's spectacles off.

"I want to be a friend of Allah, Mr. Ali. If I am a Muslim, will Allah be my friend?" asked Uthman.

"Yes, of course," Mr. Ali said, "We DO talk to Allah every time we pray to Him. Just as He always sees us, He always hears us and listens to us. He listens to our prayers when we talk to Him."

"But which language does Allah understand? We can only speak English and Arabic," asked Imran, looking at Uthman who had been thinking the same question but decided to let Imran ask all the questions in case he asked something stupid.

Mr. Ali looked at both boys and smiled at them, saying, "But Allah created everything including all the languages. Of course He knows and understands everything, every language. He understands you whether you speak German, French, Urdu, Chinese or Dutch. He knows them all." He said this to put the boys at ease.

When they understood this, they realised that they could freely and easily talk in prayer to Allah any time they wanted to. They both realised that the first thing they wanted to ask Him, was to forgive them for coming into Mr. Ali's garden without permission.

After Mr. Ali had finished telling the boys about Allah, they both apologised to him for coming into his garden and plucking his apples without permission.

But Mr. Ali said, "I've been so pleased for your visit. I'd be very happy if you would come to visit me again very often. Take some apples with you and share with your brother and sister."

The boys thanked him for his kindness and told him that they would go home to ask Allah to forgive them for what they had done.

"I'm sure Allah will forgive you," said Mr. Ali, "You didn't really know that you were doing something wrong. Allah forgives those who promise never to do, what they did wrong, again." He patted them on their heads and they left him to go home.

On their way home, Imran and Uthman worked together on composing a little poem about Allah. It went like this:

Allahu Akbar, Allah is Great,
Everything around us did He create,
He is Most Powerful and He is Most Wise,
He has control over the earth and the skies.
So we should be thankful to Allah alone
For our family, our friends, our health and our home
We should worship Allah and be good to all
For Allah knows our actions, big or small.
Allah is our protector, our helper and our friend
We should pray to Him and only on Him depend.

Quick Quiz

1) Name as many things as you can that Allah has made.

2) Does Allah have a brother or sister or mother or father? Why not?

3) How many names or qualities does Allah have?

4) How many pillars of Islam are there? Can you name at least two of the pillars of Islam.

5) Can you remember how we can be good Muslims?